Table of Contents

Chapter 1: Introduction to AI in Cybersecurity

Overview of AI in Cybersecurity

In recent years, artificial intelligence (AI) has become a game-changer in the field of cybersecurity. This subchapter provides an overview of how AI is revolutionizing the way security professionals defend against cyber threats. By harnessing the power of AI, security professionals can enhance their threat detection and prevention capabilities, streamline incident response and remediation processes, and improve security analytics and monitoring.

One of the key benefits of AI in cybersecurity is its ability to power advanced threat detection and prevention systems. AI algorithms can analyze vast amounts of data in real-time to identify patterns and anomalies that may indicate a potential security threat. By leveraging AI-powered threat detection solutions, security professionals can stay one step ahead of cyber attackers and proactively defend their digital assets.

In addition to threat detection, AI is also transforming incident response and remediation efforts. AI-driven incident response systems can automatically detect and contain security incidents, minimizing the impact of cyber attacks and reducing response times. By automating repetitive tasks and providing real-time insights, AI enables security professionals to respond to security incidents more effectively and efficiently.

Furthermore, AI-based security analytics and monitoring tools are helping security professionals gain deeper insights into their organization's security posture. By analyzing data from multiple sources and correlating information in real-time, AI-powered security analytics platforms can identify potential vulnerabilities and threats before they escalate into full-blown security incidents. This proactive approach to security monitoring enables organizations to strengthen their defenses and mitigate risks more effectively.

Moreover, AI is playing a crucial role in malware detection and removal. AI algorithms can analyze the behavior of malware samples and identify malicious code patterns, enabling security professionals to quickly detect and remove threats from their systems. By leveraging AI for malware detection and removal, organizations can minimize the impact of malware attacks and protect their sensitive data from unauthorized access.

In conclusion, AI is reshaping the landscape of cybersecurity by empowering security professionals with advanced tools and technologies to defend against evolving cyber threats. From network security and intrusion detection to phishing prevention and security compliance, AI is driving innovation across all areas of cybersecurity. By embracing AI-powered solutions, security professionals can enhance their security posture, improve incident response capabilities, and protect their organization's digital assets from malicious actors.

Importance of AI-powered threat detection and prevention

In today's digital landscape, the threat of cyber attacks is more prevalent than ever before. As security professionals, it is crucial to stay ahead of these threats and ensure the protection of sensitive data and information. This is where AI-powered threat detection and prevention comes into play, providing a proactive approach to cybersecurity that can help mitigate risks and defend against potential attacks.

AI in cybersecurity is revolutionizing the way organizations approach threat detection and prevention. By leveraging machine learning algorithms and data analytics, AI can quickly identify patterns and anomalies in network traffic, allowing for the early detection of potential threats. This proactive approach can significantly reduce the time it takes to identify and respond to security incidents, ultimately minimizing the impact of a cyber attack.

One of the key benefits of AI-powered threat detection and prevention is its ability to continuously adapt and learn from new threats. Traditional security measures rely on known signatures and patterns, making them less effective against evolving and sophisticated attacks. AI, on the other hand, can analyze vast amounts of data in real-time and identify potential threats based on behavior and context, enabling security professionals to stay one step ahead of cyber criminals.

AI-driven incident response and remediation is another important aspect of AI-powered threat detection and prevention. By automating the response to security incidents, organizations can quickly contain and mitigate the impact of a breach, reducing the risk of data loss and downtime. This not only saves time and resources but also improves the overall security posture of the organization.

In conclusion, AI-powered threat detection and prevention is essential for security professionals looking to defend against the ever-evolving threat landscape. By leveraging the power of AI in cybersecurity, organizations can strengthen their security defenses, minimize the risk of cyber attacks, and ensure the protection of critical data and information. It is imperative for security professionals to embrace AI technology and incorporate it into their cybersecurity strategies to stay ahead of potential threats and safeguard their digital assets.

Role of AI-driven incident response and remediation

In the ever-evolving landscape of cybersecurity, AI-driven incident response and remediation play a crucial role in detecting and mitigating threats in real-time. By leveraging artificial intelligence technologies, security professionals can automate the process of identifying and responding to security incidents, significantly reducing response times and minimizing the impact of cyber attacks.

One of the key advantages of AI-driven incident response is its ability to analyze vast amounts of data at speeds far beyond human capabilities. This allows security professionals to quickly identify potential threats and take proactive measures to remediate them before they escalate into full-blown security breaches. By utilizing AI-powered threat detection and prevention tools, organizations can stay one step ahead of cybercriminals and protect their sensitive data and systems from malicious attacks.

Furthermore, AI-driven incident response can also help security professionals streamline their remediation efforts by automating repetitive tasks and standardizing response procedures. This not only improves the efficiency of incident response teams but also ensures a consistent and coordinated approach to handling security incidents across the organization. By deploying AI-based security analytics and monitoring tools, security professionals can gain valuable insights into the nature and scope of security incidents, enabling them to make informed decisions on how best to respond.

In addition to enhancing incident response capabilities, AI-powered technologies can also play a crucial role in malware detection and removal, network security and intrusion detection, phishing detection and prevention, authentication and access control, security compliance and regulation, cloud security, and data protection. By integrating AI-driven solutions into their cybersecurity arsenal, organizations can better protect their digital assets and infrastructure from a wide range of cyber threats.

Ultimately, the role of AI-driven incident response and remediation in cybersecurity cannot be overstated. As cyber attacks become more sophisticated and pervasive, security professionals must embrace AI technologies to enhance their ability to detect, respond to, and mitigate security incidents effectively. By harnessing the power of AI, organizations can fortify their defenses and safeguard their critical assets against the ever-growing threat of cybercrime.

Benefits of AI-based security analytics and monitoring

In the modern digital landscape, the use of artificial intelligence (AI) in cybersecurity has become increasingly prevalent. One of the key areas where AI has made a significant impact is in security analytics and monitoring. By leveraging AI-powered tools and technologies, security professionals can enhance their ability to detect and respond to cyber threats in real-time, ultimately improving the overall security posture of their organization.

One of the primary benefits of using AI-based security analytics and monitoring is the ability to detect and respond to threats at a much faster pace than traditional methods. AI algorithms can analyze vast amounts of data and identify patterns and anomalies that may indicate a potential security threat. This proactive approach enables security teams to quickly identify and mitigate potential risks before they escalate into full-blown security incidents.

Furthermore, AI-based security analytics and monitoring can help security professionals stay ahead of evolving threats. By continuously learning and adapting to new types of cyber threats, AI-powered tools can provide security teams with real-time insights into emerging threats and vulnerabilities. This proactive approach allows organizations to better protect their sensitive data and resources from the latest cyber threats.

Another key benefit of AI-based security analytics and monitoring is the ability to automate repetitive tasks and processes. By automating routine security tasks, such as log analysis and incident response, security teams can free up valuable time and resources to focus on more strategic security initiatives. This increased efficiency can help organizations improve their overall security posture and reduce the time it takes to detect and respond to security incidents.

Additionally, AI-based security analytics and monitoring can help organizations improve their overall security compliance and regulation efforts. By leveraging AI-powered tools to monitor and analyze security events and incidents, organizations can ensure that they are meeting regulatory requirements and industry standards. This proactive approach can help organizations avoid costly fines and penalties for non-compliance, ultimately reducing the overall risk of a security breach.

In conclusion, the benefits of AI-based security analytics and monitoring are clear. By leveraging AI-powered tools and technologies, security professionals can enhance their ability to detect and respond to cyber threats in real-time, stay ahead of evolving threats, automate repetitive tasks, and improve security compliance and regulation efforts. Ultimately, AI-based security analytics and monitoring can help organizations strengthen their overall security posture and better protect their sensitive data and resources from cyber threats.

Chapter 2: AI in Malware Detection and Removal

Understanding AI in malware detection

Malware detection is a critical component of cybersecurity, as malicious software can wreak havoc on computer systems and compromise sensitive data. Traditional methods of detecting malware involve signature-based detection, in which known malware signatures are compared against files on the system. However, as cyber threats continue to evolve and become more sophisticated, traditional methods are no longer sufficient to defend against them. This is where artificial intelligence (AI) comes in.

AI-powered malware detection systems leverage machine learning algorithms to analyze patterns and behaviors in order to identify and neutralize malware in real time. These systems are capable of continuously learning and adapting to new threats, making them far more effective at detecting previously unknown malware variants. By using AI in malware detection, security professionals can stay one step ahead of cyber attackers and protect their systems from the latest threats.

One key advantage of using AI in malware detection is its ability to detect zero-day attacks, which are attacks that exploit previously unknown vulnerabilities. Traditional antivirus software may not be able to detect zero-day attacks because they rely on known signatures to identify malware. AI-powered malware detection systems, on the other hand, can detect zero-day attacks by analyzing the behavior of files and processes on the system, rather than relying on signatures.

AI-driven malware detection systems can also reduce false positives, which are alerts that incorrectly identify legitimate files as malware. By using machine learning algorithms to analyze file behavior and characteristics, AI-powered systems can more accurately distinguish between legitimate files and malware. This reduces the burden on security professionals, allowing them to focus on genuine threats and respond more effectively.

In conclusion, AI has revolutionized malware detection by enabling security professionals to detect and respond to threats in real time. By leveraging machine learning algorithms, AI-powered malware detection systems can identify and neutralize malware before it can cause damage to computer systems. With the constantly evolving threat landscape, AI in malware detection is essential for security professionals to stay ahead of cyber attackers and protect their organizations' critical assets.

Implementing AI for malware removal

Implementing AI for malware removal is a crucial aspect of cybersecurity for security professionals. With the increasing sophistication of malware attacks, traditional methods of detection and removal are no longer sufficient to protect organizations from advanced threats. AI-powered malware removal tools are essential for identifying and eliminating malicious software before it can cause damage to critical systems and data.

One of the key benefits of using AI for malware removal is its ability to quickly analyze large volumes of data to identify patterns and anomalies that may indicate the presence of malware. Traditional signature-based antivirus programs are limited in their effectiveness against new and unknown threats, but AI algorithms can adapt and learn from new data to stay ahead of cybercriminals.

AI-powered threat detection and prevention tools can also help security professionals to automate the process of identifying and removing malware, reducing the time and resources required to respond to incidents. By using machine learning algorithms to continuously monitor network traffic and systems for suspicious activity, AI can proactively detect and block malware before it can spread and cause damage.

In addition to detecting and preventing malware attacks, AI-driven incident response and remediation tools can help security professionals to quickly contain and mitigate the impact of a security breach. By automating the process of isolating infected systems, removing malware, and restoring affected data, AI can help organizations to minimize downtime and reduce the cost of recovering from a cyberattack.

Overall, implementing AI for malware removal is essential for security professionals to effectively protect their organizations from the growing threat of malware attacks. By leveraging the power of AI algorithms to detect, prevent, and respond to malicious software, security professionals can strengthen their defenses and stay one step ahead of cybercriminals.

Chapter 3: AI for Network Security and Intrusion Detection

Utilizing AI for network security

Utilizing AI for network security is an innovative approach that is revolutionizing the way security professionals protect their organizations from cyber threats. With the increasing complexity and volume of cyber attacks, traditional security measures are no longer sufficient. AI-powered solutions have the ability to analyze vast amounts of data in real-time, identify patterns and anomalies, and proactively detect and respond to security incidents.

One of the key benefits of AI for network security is its ability to enhance threat detection and prevention. By continuously monitoring network traffic and behavior, AI algorithms can quickly identify suspicious activities and potential security breaches. This proactive approach enables security professionals to take action before a threat escalates, reducing the risk of a successful cyber attack.

In addition to threat detection, AI-driven incident response and remediation capabilities are essential for effective network security.

When a security incident occurs, AI-powered systems can automatically isolate infected devices, contain the spread of malware, and remediate the issue in real-time. This swift response helps minimize the impact of a security breach and prevent further damage to the network.

AI-based security analytics and monitoring play a crucial role in network security by providing security professionals with valuable insights into the organization's security posture. By analyzing data from various sources, AI algorithms can identify vulnerabilities, assess risks, and prioritize security tasks. This proactive approach enables security teams to focus their efforts on the most critical security issues, ultimately strengthening the organization's overall security posture.

Overall, leveraging AI for network security enables security professionals to stay ahead of evolving cyber threats and protect their organizations from sophisticated attacks. By harnessing the power of AI for threat detection, incident response, security analytics, and monitoring, security professionals can enhance their capabilities, improve their efficiency, and ensure the security of their networks in today's rapidly evolving threat landscape.

Enhancing intrusion detection with AI

Enhancing intrusion detection with AI can significantly improve the effectiveness and efficiency of cybersecurity measures for security professionals. By leveraging AI technology, security teams can better detect and respond to cyber threats in real-time, helping to prevent potentially devastating data breaches. AI-powered threat detection and prevention systems can quickly identify and analyze suspicious activities, enabling security professionals to take immediate action to mitigate risks.

AI-driven incident response and remediation capabilities can streamline the process of resolving security incidents, reducing the time it takes to contain and remediate threats. With AI-based security analytics and monitoring tools, security professionals can gain valuable insights into potential vulnerabilities and threats within their network, allowing them to proactively address security gaps before they are exploited by malicious actors.

AI in malware detection and removal is another key area where AI technology can enhance intrusion detection capabilities. By using machine learning algorithms to identify and quarantine malware, security professionals can quickly neutralize threats and protect sensitive data from being compromised. Additionally, AI for network security and intrusion detection can help to detect and block unauthorized access attempts, ensuring that only authorized users can access critical systems and data.

AI in phishing detection and prevention is crucial for safeguarding against social engineering attacks that target unsuspecting employees. By using AI-powered algorithms to analyze email communications and identify suspicious phishing attempts, security professionals can prevent employees from falling victim to phishing scams. Furthermore, AI-powered authentication and access control systems can enhance security measures by using biometric data and behavioral analytics to verify user identities and prevent unauthorized access to sensitive information.

In conclusion, implementing AI technology in cybersecurity practices can help security professionals enhance their intrusion detection capabilities and bolster their overall cybersecurity defenses. By leveraging AI-driven security automation and orchestration tools, security teams can automate routine security tasks and respond to cyber threats more effectively. Additionally, AI can assist with security compliance and regulation by ensuring that organizations adhere to industry standards and best practices. Overall, AI in cybersecurity is a powerful tool for security professionals looking to protect their organizations from evolving cyber threats and safeguard sensitive data.

Chapter 4: AI in Phishing Detection and Prevention

The impact of AI in phishing detection

Phishing attacks have long been a major concern for cybersecurity professionals, as they continue to be a prevalent threat to organizations of all sizes. With the advancement of artificial intelligence (AI) technology, however, there is hope for more effective detection and prevention of these malicious attacks. In this subchapter, we will explore the impact of AI in phishing detection and how it is revolutionizing the way organizations defend against this type of cyber threat.

One of the key ways in which AI is transforming phishing detection is through its ability to analyze vast amounts of data in real-time. Traditional methods of detecting phishing attacks often rely on static rules and signatures, which can be easily bypassed by sophisticated attackers. AI, on the other hand, can learn from patterns and anomalies in data to detect phishing emails that may otherwise go unnoticed. By continuously analyzing and adapting to new threats, AI-powered systems are able to stay ahead of cybercriminals and protect organizations from falling victim to phishing scams.

Another important aspect of AI in phishing detection is its ability to automate the response to suspected attacks. When a phishing email is detected, AI can automatically quarantine the email, alert security professionals, and even take action to prevent further spread of the attack. This not only saves time and resources for security teams but also ensures a swift response to minimize the impact of the phishing campaign.

Furthermore, AI can enhance security analytics and monitoring by providing valuable insights into phishing trends and patterns. By analyzing data from past phishing attacks, AI can identify common characteristics and behaviors associated with these types of campaigns, allowing security professionals to proactively defend against future threats. This proactive approach to cybersecurity is crucial in today's rapidly evolving threat landscape, where cybercriminals are constantly developing new tactics to bypass traditional security measures.

In conclusion, the impact of AI in phishing detection cannot be overstated. By leveraging AI technology, organizations can strengthen their defenses against phishing attacks and reduce the risk of falling victim to these malicious campaigns. As security professionals, it is essential to embrace AI-powered tools and systems for more effective threat detection and prevention in the fight against cybercrime. By staying informed and adopting best practices in AI cybersecurity, organizations can stay ahead of cyber threats and protect their valuable assets from potential harm.

Strategies for AI-powered phishing prevention

Phishing attacks continue to be a major threat to organizations of all sizes, with cybercriminals becoming increasingly sophisticated in their tactics. As security professionals, it is essential to leverage the power of artificial intelligence (AI) to prevent these potentially devastating attacks. In this subchapter, we will explore strategies for AI-powered phishing prevention to help you defend your organization's digital frontier.

One of the key strategies for AI-powered phishing prevention is the use of machine learning algorithms to analyze email content and identify suspicious patterns. By training these algorithms on a large dataset of known phishing emails, AI can quickly detect and flag potential threats before they reach the inbox of unsuspecting employees. This proactive approach can significantly reduce the risk of successful phishing attacks and help to protect sensitive information.

Another important strategy is the use of AI-powered link analysis to identify malicious URLs in emails. Cybercriminals often use phishing emails to trick recipients into clicking on links that lead to fake websites designed to steal login credentials or other sensitive data. AI can analyze the structure and content of URLs to determine if they are legitimate or malicious, providing an additional layer of defense against phishing attacks.

In addition to analyzing email content and links, AI can also be used to monitor user behavior and detect anomalies that may indicate a phishing attempt. By establishing baseline behavior patterns for individual users,

AI algorithms can identify deviations that suggest a user has been compromised or is being targeted by a phishing attack. This real-time monitoring can help security teams respond quickly to potential threats and mitigate the impact of phishing attacks.

Furthermore, AI-powered phishing prevention can be enhanced through the integration of threat intelligence feeds and data from other security tools. By combining information from multiple sources, AI can provide a more comprehensive view of potential threats and help security professionals make more informed decisions about how to respond. This holistic approach to phishing prevention can strengthen your organization's defenses and improve overall cybersecurity posture.

In conclusion, AI offers powerful capabilities for preventing phishing attacks and protecting critical data from cyber threats. By leveraging machine learning algorithms, link analysis, user behavior monitoring, and threat intelligence integration, security professionals can enhance their organization's defenses against phishing attacks. By staying informed about the latest AI technologies and best practices for phishing prevention, you can help safeguard your organization's digital assets and maintain a strong security posture in the face of evolving cyber threats.

Chapter 5: AI-powered Authentication and Access Control

Enhancing security with AI-based authentication

Enhancing security with AI-based authentication is a crucial aspect of modern cybersecurity measures. As security professionals, it is essential to stay ahead of the curve and utilize the latest technologies to protect sensitive data and systems. AI-powered authentication offers a more robust and efficient way to verify user identities and prevent unauthorized access to networks and applications.

One of the key benefits of AI-based authentication is its ability to adapt to changing threats and patterns. Traditional authentication methods such as passwords and security questions are no longer sufficient in today's rapidly evolving threat landscape. AI algorithms can analyze user behavior, biometric data, and other factors to create a unique authentication profile for each individual, making it much harder for cybercriminals to bypass security measures.

Moreover, AI-based authentication can also help streamline the user experience by reducing the number of steps required to verify identities. By leveraging machine learning algorithms, security professionals can implement seamless authentication processes that do not disrupt the user workflow while still maintaining high levels of security. This is especially important in environments where users need to access multiple systems and applications regularly.

Additionally, AI-powered authentication can provide real-time insights into potential security threats and anomalies. By continuously monitoring user behavior and access patterns, AI algorithms can quickly detect suspicious activities and flag them for further investigation. This proactive approach to security can help security professionals identify and mitigate potential risks before they escalate into full-blown security incidents.

In conclusion, AI-based authentication is a powerful tool for enhancing security measures in today's digital landscape. By leveraging the latest advancements in artificial intelligence, security professionals can create more robust and efficient authentication processes that protect sensitive data and systems from cyber threats. As the cybersecurity industry continues to evolve, integrating AI into authentication strategies will be essential for staying ahead of malicious actors and safeguarding critical assets.

Implementing AI for access control

Implementing AI for access control is a crucial aspect of cybersecurity for security professionals. By utilizing artificial intelligence in access control systems, organizations can enhance their security measures and protect sensitive data from unauthorized access. AI-powered authentication and access control systems use advanced algorithms to analyze user behavior and determine if access should be granted or denied based on risk factors.

One of the key benefits of implementing AI for access control is the ability to detect suspicious behavior and potential security threats in real-time. AI algorithms can quickly identify anomalies in user activity and trigger alerts for security teams to investigate further. This proactive approach to access control can help prevent data breaches and unauthorized access before they occur, minimizing the impact on the organization.

Furthermore, AI-powered access control systems can adapt to evolving security threats and adjust access permissions dynamically. By continuously learning and improving from data inputs, AI algorithms can make informed decisions about access rights based on the latest threat intelligence. This adaptive approach to access control is essential in today's rapidly changing cybersecurity landscape, where traditional rule-based systems may be insufficient to keep pace with emerging threats.

In addition, AI for access control can streamline the authentication process for users, enhancing the user experience while maintaining security standards. By leveraging AI algorithms for user authentication, organizations can implement multi-factor authentication methods that are both secure and user-friendly. This balance between security and usability is crucial in ensuring that employees can access the resources they need efficiently while maintaining robust security measures.

Overall, implementing AI for access control is a strategic investment for organizations looking to bolster their cybersecurity defenses. By harnessing the power of artificial intelligence in access control systems, security professionals can enhance their threat detection capabilities, improve incident response times, and strengthen overall security posture. With AI-driven access control, organizations can effectively protect their digital assets and mitigate the risks associated with unauthorized access.

Chapter 6: AI for Security Compliance and Regulation

Ensuring compliance with AI

In the fast-paced world of cybersecurity, ensuring compliance with AI is crucial for security professionals. As AI continues to play a significant role in threat detection, incident response, security analytics, and more, it is essential to understand how to effectively implement and manage these technologies in compliance with industry regulations and standards.

One key aspect of ensuring compliance with AI in cybersecurity is understanding the legal and ethical implications of using AI-powered tools. Security professionals must stay up to date on the latest laws and regulations surrounding AI, as well as ethical considerations such as data privacy and bias in AI algorithms. By ensuring that AI tools are used ethically and legally, security professionals can avoid potential legal pitfalls and maintain the trust of their stakeholders.

Another important consideration for compliance with AI in cybersecurity is ensuring that AI tools are properly configured and monitored. Security professionals must have a thorough understanding of how AI algorithms work and be able to validate the results they produce. By regularly monitoring and auditing AI systems, security professionals can ensure that they are functioning as intended and compliant with industry standards.

Additionally, security professionals must ensure that AI tools are integrated into existing security processes and technologies in a compliant manner. This includes ensuring that AI-powered threat detection and prevention tools work seamlessly with existing security systems, as well as ensuring that AI-driven incident response and remediation processes are aligned with industry best practices. By integrating AI tools effectively, security professionals can maximize their effectiveness while maintaining compliance with relevant regulations.

Overall, ensuring compliance with AI in cybersecurity requires a proactive approach that considers legal, ethical, and technical considerations. By staying informed on the latest regulations and standards, monitoring and auditing AI systems, and integrating AI tools effectively, security professionals can harness the power of AI while maintaining compliance with industry regulations and standards. By taking a proactive approach to compliance with AI, security professionals can stay ahead of potential risks and protect their organizations from cyber threats.

Adhering to security regulations with AI

When it comes to cybersecurity, adhering to security regulations is crucial in order to protect sensitive data and prevent cyber attacks. With the advancement of artificial intelligence (AI) technology, security professionals now have powerful tools at their disposal to help ensure compliance with security regulations.

AI in cybersecurity plays a significant role in threat detection and prevention. By leveraging AI-powered algorithms, security professionals can identify and mitigate potential threats in real-time, reducing the risk of cyber attacks. This proactive approach to cybersecurity is essential in today's constantly evolving threat landscape.

In addition to threat detection, AI-driven incident response and remediation tools can help security professionals effectively respond to security incidents. By automating the incident response process, AI can help minimize the impact of a security breach and reduce the time it takes to remediate the issue. This rapid response is essential in preventing further damage and protecting sensitive data.

AI-based security analytics and monitoring tools are also essential in ensuring compliance with security regulations. By analyzing large volumes of data in real-time, AI can identify patterns and anomalies that may indicate a security threat. This proactive approach to monitoring can help security professionals stay ahead of potential threats and maintain compliance with security regulations.

Overall, integrating AI into cybersecurity practices can help security professionals adhere to security regulations more effectively. From threat detection and prevention to incident response and remediation, AI has the potential to revolutionize the way security professionals protect sensitive data and prevent cyber attacks. By leveraging AI technology, security professionals can stay one step ahead of cybercriminals and ensure compliance with security regulations.

Chapter 7: AI in Cloud Security and Data Protection

Securing cloud environments with AI

Securing cloud environments with AI is becoming increasingly crucial in today's digital landscape. As more organizations move their data and applications to the cloud, the need for robust security measures has never been greater. AI-powered tools and technologies offer a powerful way to enhance cloud security and protect sensitive information from cyber threats.

One of the key benefits of using AI in cloud security is its ability to detect and prevent threats in real-time. AI algorithms can analyze vast amounts of data and identify suspicious patterns or anomalies that could indicate a potential security breach. By continuously monitoring cloud environments, AI can proactively identify and mitigate security risks before they escalate into full-blown attacks.

In addition to threat detection and prevention, AI-driven incident response and remediation can help organizations quickly respond to security incidents and minimize their impact. AI-powered tools can automatically isolate compromised systems, contain the spread of malware, and remediate vulnerabilities to prevent future attacks. This rapid response capability is essential for minimizing downtime and protecting critical data in cloud environments.

AI-based security analytics and monitoring are also essential for maintaining visibility into cloud environments and detecting unauthorized access or suspicious activities. By analyzing network traffic, user behavior, and application logs, AI can identify potential security threats and provide security professionals with valuable insights to strengthen their defenses. This proactive approach to security monitoring can help organizations stay one step ahead of cybercriminals and prevent data breaches.

Moreover, AI can enhance cloud security and data protection by automating routine security tasks, such as malware detection and removal, phishing detection and prevention, authentication and access control, and security compliance and regulation. By leveraging AI-powered automation and orchestration, security professionals can streamline their security operations, reduce human error, and respond to security incidents more efficiently. This level of automation is essential for managing the complexity of cloud environments and ensuring consistent security across all cloud assets.

Protecting data using AI

In the ever-evolving landscape of cybersecurity, protecting data is of utmost importance for security professionals. With the increasing sophistication of cyber threats, traditional security measures are no longer sufficient. This is where artificial intelligence (AI) comes into play, offering advanced capabilities for detecting and preventing security breaches.

AI-powered threat detection and prevention systems are able to analyze vast amounts of data in real-time, identifying patterns and anomalies that may indicate a potential attack. By leveraging machine learning algorithms, these systems can continuously adapt and improve their detection capabilities, staying one step ahead of cybercriminals. This proactive approach is essential for defending against today's advanced threats.

In the event of a security incident, AI-driven incident response and remediation tools can help security professionals quickly contain and mitigate the damage. These tools can automate the response process, reducing the time it takes to identify and address threats. By streamlining incident response workflows, AI can help organizations minimize the impact of security breaches and prevent further damage to their systems and data.

AI-based security analytics and monitoring tools provide security professionals with real-time insights into their organization's security posture. By analyzing data from various sources, including network traffic, logs, and endpoints, these tools can identify potential security risks and vulnerabilities. This proactive approach allows security teams to take preemptive action to protect their data and systems from potential threats.

AI in malware detection and removal is another crucial aspect of protecting data. Traditional antivirus solutions are no longer sufficient to defend against the rapidly evolving threat landscape. AI-powered malware detection tools can detect and remove malicious software more effectively, reducing the risk of data breaches and other cyber attacks. By leveraging AI algorithms, security professionals can stay ahead of malware threats and keep their systems secure.

Chapter 8: AI-driven Security Automation and Orchestration

Automating security processes with AI

In today's rapidly evolving digital landscape, cybersecurity professionals are constantly facing new and sophisticated threats. Traditional security measures are no longer enough to defend against these advanced cyber-attacks. This is where the integration of artificial intelligence (AI) into cybersecurity processes becomes crucial. By automating security processes with AI, professionals can enhance their ability to detect, prevent, respond to, and remediate threats in real-time.

AI-powered threat detection and prevention is one of the key areas where security professionals can leverage the power of AI. Machine learning algorithms can analyze vast amounts of data to identify patterns and anomalies that may indicate a potential threat. By continuously learning from new data, AI can improve its threat detection capabilities over time, staying one step ahead of cybercriminals.

When it comes to incident response and remediation, AI can streamline the process by automating the identification and containment of security incidents. By using AI-driven incident response tools, security professionals can quickly assess the scope and severity of an incident and take immediate action to mitigate the damage. This not only reduces response times but also minimizes the impact of security breaches on an organization.

AI-based security analytics and monitoring are essential for proactive threat intelligence. By analyzing network traffic, user behavior, and system logs in real-time, AI can identify suspicious activities and potential security risks before they escalate into full-blown attacks. This continuous monitoring ensures that security professionals are always aware of the latest threats and can take preemptive measures to protect their networks.

In addition to threat detection and incident response, AI can also play a critical role in malware detection and removal. By using AI algorithms to analyze the behavior of files and applications, security professionals can quickly identify and quarantine malicious software before it can cause harm. This proactive approach to malware detection is essential for keeping systems safe from the ever-evolving tactics of cybercriminals.

Overall, automating security processes with AI is essential for security professionals to stay ahead of the curve in today's cyber threat landscape. By leveraging the power of AI for network security and intrusion detection, phishing detection and prevention, authentication and access control, compliance and regulation, cloud security, and data protection, professionals can enhance their ability to defend against cyber-attacks and protect their organizations' valuable data and assets. With AI-driven security automation and orchestration, professionals can streamline their security operations, improve their response times, and ultimately strengthen their overall cybersecurity posture.

Orchestrating security measures using AI

In the rapidly evolving landscape of cybersecurity, artificial intelligence (AI) has emerged as a powerful tool for orchestrating security measures. By harnessing the capabilities of AI, security professionals can enhance their ability to detect and prevent threats, respond to incidents, analyze and monitor security data, detect and remove malware, secure networks, prevent phishing attacks, control access, ensure compliance with regulations, protect data in the cloud, and automate security processes.

AI-powered threat detection and prevention have revolutionized the way security professionals approach cybersecurity. By leveraging machine learning algorithms, AI can analyze vast amounts of data in real-time to identify patterns and anomalies that may indicate a potential threat. This proactive approach allows security teams to stay one step ahead of cybercriminals and prevent attacks before they can cause harm.

When it comes to incident response and remediation, AI-driven solutions can significantly streamline the process. By automating the detection, analysis, and containment of security incidents, AI can help security professionals respond more quickly and effectively to threats. This not only reduces the impact of security breaches but also minimizes the time and resources required to resolve them.

In the realm of security analytics and monitoring, AI can provide invaluable insights into the security posture of an organization. By continuously analyzing security data and generating actionable intelligence, AI can help security professionals identify vulnerabilities, prioritize risks, and make informed decisions to strengthen their defenses. This proactive approach is essential in today's fast-paced cybersecurity landscape.

AI is also instrumental in malware detection and removal, as it can identify and neutralize threats in real-time. By leveraging AI-powered tools, security professionals can detect and eradicate malware before it can spread and cause damage. This proactive approach is crucial in protecting sensitive data and ensuring the integrity of an organization's systems.

Overall, AI has the potential to revolutionize every aspect of cybersecurity, from network security and intrusion detection to phishing prevention, access control, compliance, and cloud security. By harnessing the power of AI, security professionals can enhance their ability to defend the digital frontier and stay ahead of cyber threats. With AI-driven security automation and orchestration, security professionals can streamline their processes, improve their efficiency, and ultimately strengthen their defenses against evolving cyber threats.

Chapter 9: Conclusion and Future Trends in AI Cybersecurity

Summary of key points

In this subchapter titled "Summary of key points," we will recap the main takeaways from the book "Defending the Digital Frontier: AI in Cybersecurity for Security Professionals." The book delves into the critical role that Artificial Intelligence (AI) plays in enhancing cybersecurity measures and protecting digital assets.

First and foremost, AI in cybersecurity offers advanced threat detection and prevention capabilities. By leveraging machine learning algorithms, AI-powered systems can analyze vast amounts of data in real-time to identify and mitigate potential security risks before they escalate into full-blown cyber attacks. This proactive approach is essential in today's rapidly evolving threat landscape.

Furthermore, AI-driven incident response and remediation are crucial components of effective cybersecurity strategies. By automating the process of detecting and responding to security incidents, organizations can significantly reduce response times and minimize the impact of security breaches. This rapid response is essential for containing threats and preventing further damage to the network.

Moreover, AI-based security analytics and monitoring provide security professionals with valuable insights into their organization's security posture. By continuously analyzing network traffic, user behavior, and system logs, AI-powered systems can identify anomalies and suspicious activities that may indicate a potential security breach. This proactive monitoring is essential for staying one step ahead of cybercriminals.

Additionally, AI in malware detection and removal is a game-changer in the fight against malicious software. Traditional antivirus solutions are no match for the sophisticated malware strains that are constantly evolving. AI-powered systems can detect and neutralize malware in real-time, protecting critical systems and data from unauthorized access and exploitation.

Lastly, AI for network security and intrusion detection, AI in phishing detection and prevention, AI-powered authentication and access control, AI for security compliance and regulation, AI in cloud security and data protection, and AI-driven security automation and orchestration are all essential areas where AI can greatly enhance cybersecurity measures. By incorporating AI into these key areas, security professionals can bolster their defenses and protect their organizations from a wide range of cyber threats.

Emerging trends in AI cybersecurity for security professionals

As security professionals continue to navigate the ever-evolving landscape of cyber threats, it is crucial to stay informed on the latest trends in AI cybersecurity. The integration of artificial intelligence (AI) in cybersecurity has revolutionized the way organizations detect, prevent, and respond to cyber attacks. In this subchapter, we will explore the emerging trends in AI cybersecurity that are shaping the future of security professionals.

One of the key trends in AI cybersecurity is AI-powered threat detection and prevention. AI algorithms can analyze vast amounts of data in real-time to identify potential threats and anomalies that may go undetected by traditional security measures. By leveraging machine learning and deep learning techniques, organizations can proactively defend against sophisticated cyber attacks and minimize the risk of data breaches.

Another important trend is AI-driven incident response and remediation. In the event of a security incident, AI technologies can automate the response process, enabling security teams to quickly contain the threat and mitigate potential damage. By streamlining incident response workflows and providing real-time insights, AI can help security professionals effectively manage security incidents and minimize downtime.

AI-based security analytics and monitoring are also gaining momentum in the cybersecurity industry. By continuously monitoring network traffic and analyzing user behavior, AI systems can detect suspicious activities and patterns that may indicate a potential security threat. This proactive approach to security monitoring enables organizations to identify and address vulnerabilities before they are exploited by cybercriminals.

AI in malware detection and removal is another emerging trend that security professionals should be aware of. Traditional antivirus software is no longer sufficient to combat the growing number of sophisticated malware attacks. AI-powered malware detection tools can identify and neutralize malware in real-time, helping organizations protect their systems and data from malicious software.

Overall, the integration of AI in cybersecurity is revolutionizing the way security professionals defend against cyber threats. By staying informed on the latest trends in AI cybersecurity, security professionals can enhance their cybersecurity strategies and better protect their organizations from evolving cyber threats. Embracing AI technologies in areas such as network security, incident response, and malware detection will be essential for staying ahead of cybercriminals and safeguarding sensitive data.